easy **GUITAR** play along

ROCK classics

Volume 1

ISBN 978-1-4584-1577-6

HAL•LEONARD®
CORPORATION
7777 W. BLUEMOUND RD. P.O. BOX 13819 MILWAUKEE, WI 53213

Visit Hal Leonard Online at
www.halleonard.com

Guitar Notation Legend

THE MUSICAL STAFF shows pitches and rhythms and is divided by bar lines into measures. Pitches are named after the first seven letters of the alphabet.

TABLATURE graphically represents the guitar fingerboard. Each horizontal line represents a string, and each number represents a fret.

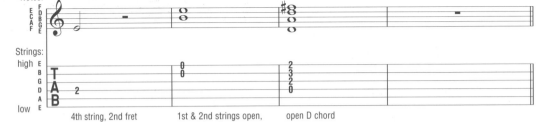

4th string, 2nd fret | 1st & 2nd strings open, played together | open D chord

HALF-STEP BEND: Strike the note and bend up 1/2 step.

WHOLE-STEP BEND: Strike the note and bend up one step.

GRACE NOTE BEND: Strike the note and immediately bend up as indicated.

SLIGHT (MICROTONE) BEND: Strike the note and bend up 1/4 step.

BEND AND RELEASE: Strike the note and bend up as indicated, then release back to the original note. Only the first note is struck.

PRE-BEND: Bend the note as indicated, then strike it.

VIBRATO: The string is vibrated by rapidly bending and releasing the note with the fretting hand.

PALM MUTING: The note is partially muted by the pick hand lightly touching the string(s) just before the bridge.

HAMMER-ON: Strike the first (lower) note with one finger, then sound the higher note (on the same string) with another finger by fretting it without picking.

PULL-OFF: Place both fingers on the notes to be sounded. Strike the first note and without picking, pull the finger off to sound the second (lower) note.

LEGATO SLIDE: Strike the first note and then slide the same fret-hand finger up or down to the second note. The second note is not struck.

SHIFT SLIDE: Same as legato slide, except the second note is struck.

TRILL: Very rapidly alternate between the notes indicated by continuously hammering on and pulling off.

TAPPING: Hammer ("tap") the fret indicated with the pick-hand index or middle finger and pull off to the note fretted by the fret hand.

NATURAL HARMONIC: Strike the note while the fret-hand lightly touches the string directly over the fret indicated.

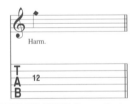

PINCH HARMONIC: The note is fretted normally and a harmonic is produced by adding the edge of the thumb or the tip of the index finger of the pick hand to the normal pick attack.

TREMOLO PICKING: The note is picked as rapidly and continuously as possible.

VIBRATO BAR DIVE AND RETURN: The pitch of the note or chord is dropped a specified number of steps (in rhythm), then returned to the original pitch.

VIBRATO BAR SCOOP: Depress the bar just before striking the note, then quickly release the bar.

VIBRATO BAR DIP: Strike the note and then immediately drop a specified number of steps, then release back to the original pitch.

Additional Musical Definitions

(accent) • Accentuate note (play it louder).

(staccato) • Play the note short.

D.S. al Coda • Go back to the sign (%), then play until the measure marked "*To Coda*," then skip to the section labelled "**Coda**."

D.C. al Fine • Go back to the beginning of the song and play until the measure marked "*Fine*" (end).

Fill • Label used to identify a brief melodic figure which is to be inserted into the arrangement.

N.C. • Harmony is implied.

• Repeat measures between signs.

• When a repeated section has different endings, play the first ending only the first time and the second ending only the second time.

Jailbreak

Words and Music by Philip Parris Lynott

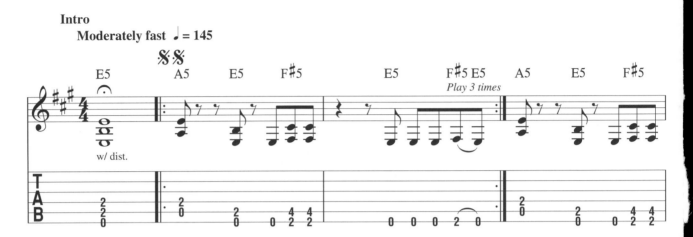

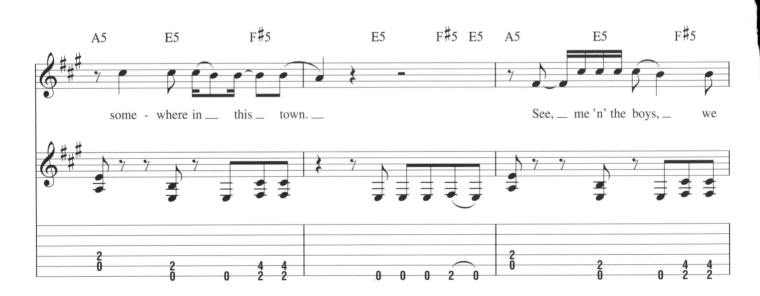

To Coda 2 ⊕

Chorus

5

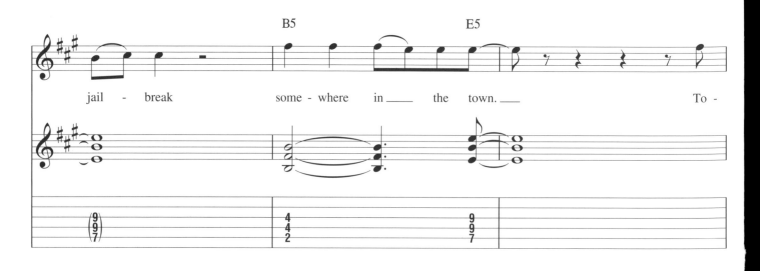

jail - break some - where in ____ the town. ____ To -

To Coda 1

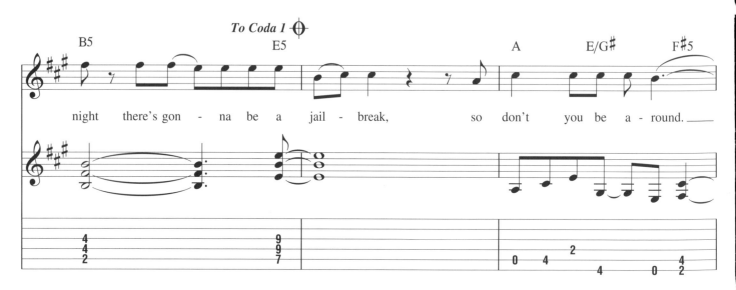

night there's gon - na be a jail - break, so don't you be a - round. ____

Interlude

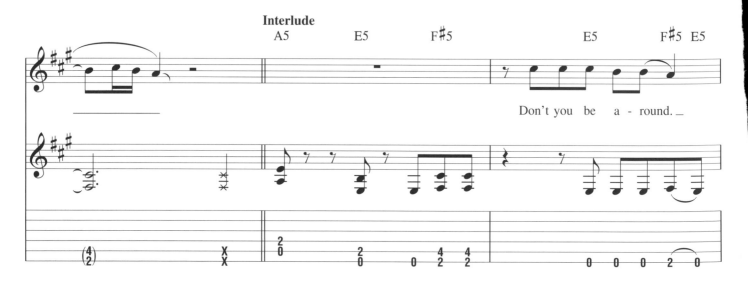

____ Don't you be a - round. _

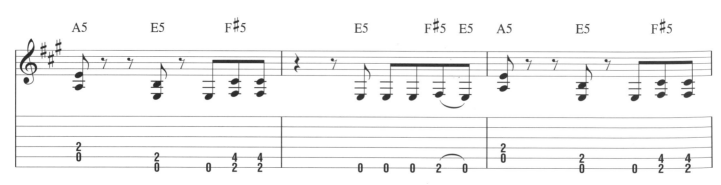

8

$\oplus$ Coda 2

Chorus

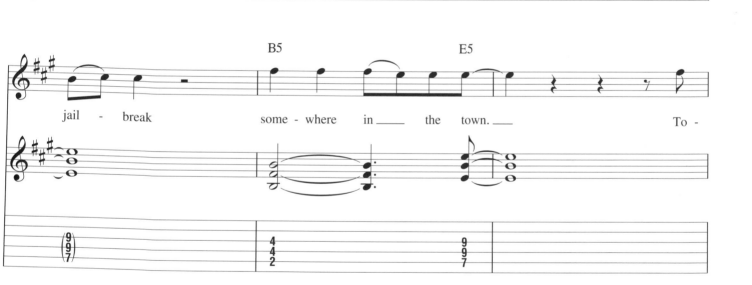

To - night there's gon - na be a

jail - break some - where in the town. To -

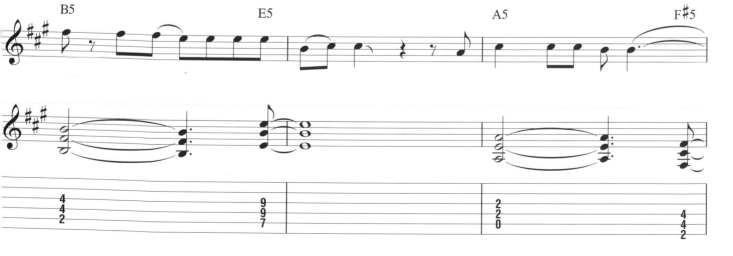

Additional Lyrics

2. Tonight there's gonna be trouble.
   Some of us won't survive.
   See, the boys and me mean business.
   Bustin' out dead or alive.
   I can hear hound dogs on my trail.
   All hell breaks loose, alarm and sirens wail.
   Like a game, if you lose, go to jail!

3. Tonight there's gonna be a breakout,
   Into the city zones.
   Don't you dare try to stop us,
   No one could for long.
   Searchlight on my trail.
   Tonight's the night, all systems fail.
   Good lookin' female, come here.

Mississippi Queen

Words and Music by Leslie West, Felix Pappalardi, Corky Laing and David Rea

2. This lady, she asked me
   If I would be her man.
   You know that I told her
   I'd do what I can
   To keep her lookin' pretty.
   Buy her dresses that shine.
   While the rest of them dudes wa a-makin' their bread;
   Buddy, beg your pardon, I was losin' mine.

Living After Midnight

Words and Music by Glenn Tipton, Rob Halford and K.K. Downing

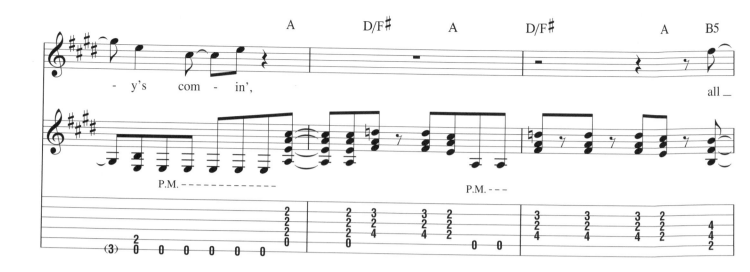

Guitar Solo

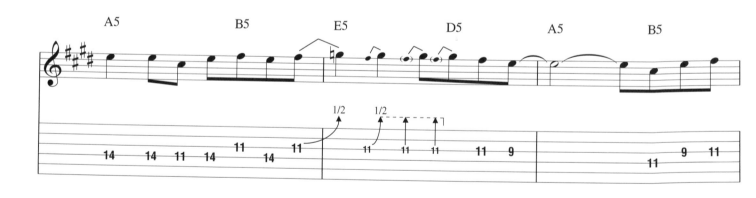

D.S. al Coda

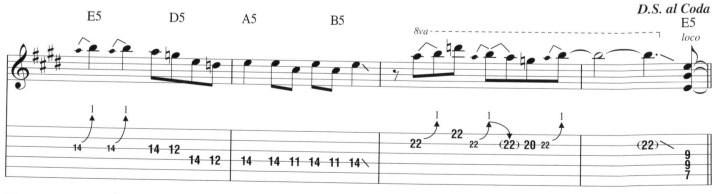

⊕ **Coda**

Outro-Chorus

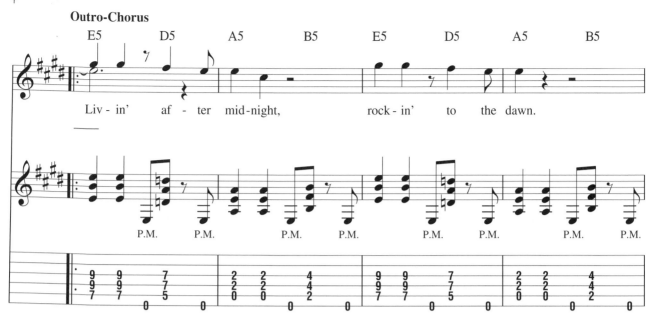

Liv - in' af - ter mid-night, rock - in' to the dawn.

Repeat and fade

Lov - in' till the morn - in', then I'm gone, ___ I'm gone. ___

Additional Lyrics

2. Got gleamin' chrome reflecting feel.
Loaded, loaded.
Ready to take on ev'ry deal.
Loaded, loaded.

Pre-Chorus 2. My pulse is racin', hot to take.
But this motor's revved up, fit to break.

Loaded, loaded.
I'm gettin' harder by the hour.
Loaded, loaded.

Pre-Chorus 3. I set my sights and then home in.
The joints start fly'n' when I begin.

Rocks Off

Words and Music by Mick Jagger and Keith Richards

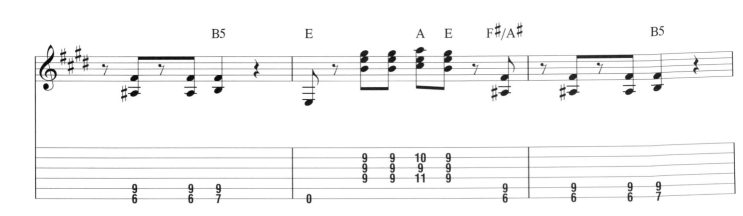

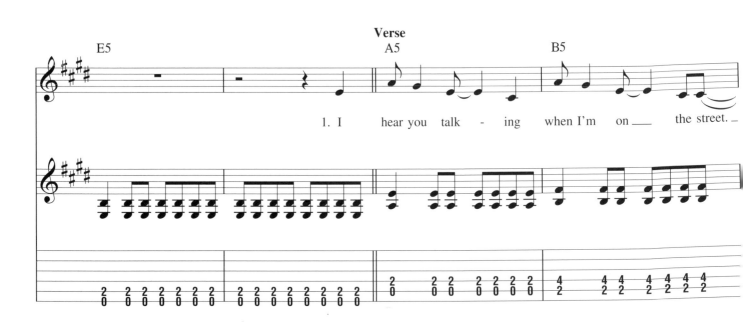

Is he gon - na close the door __ on __ me? __

𝄋 Verse

2. And I'm al - ways hear - in' voic - es on __ the street. __
3., 4. *See additional lyrics*

I want __ to shout, __ but I __

__ can't hard - ly speak. __

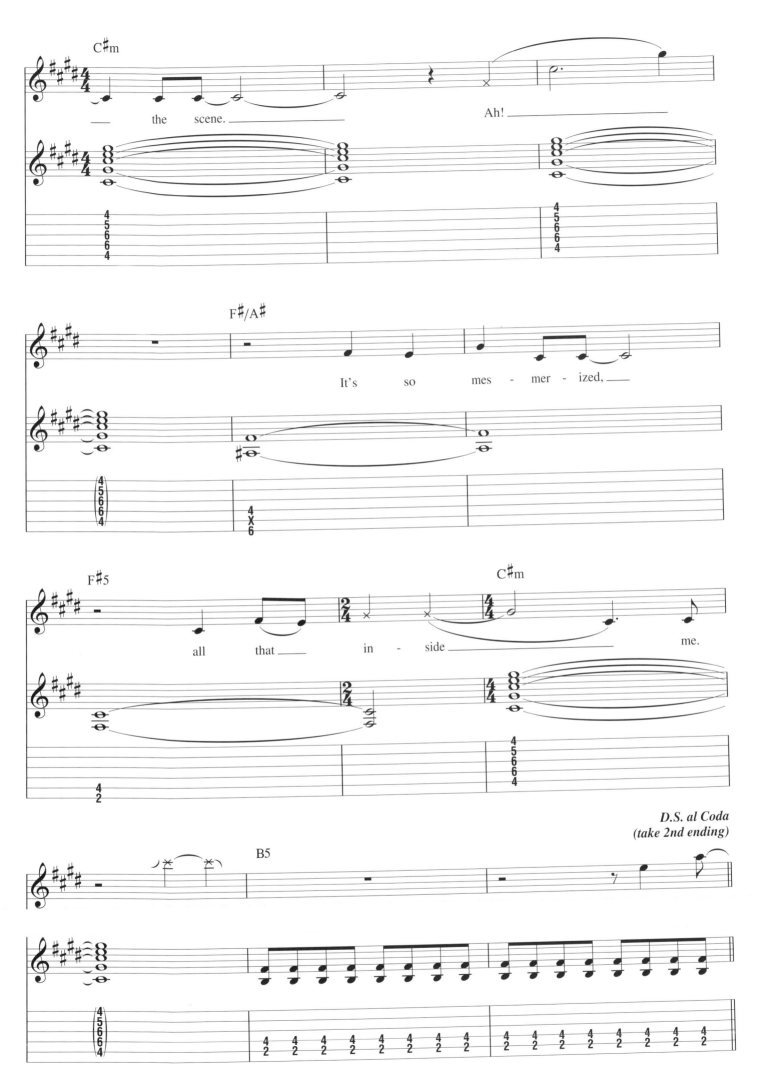

D.S. al Coda
(take 2nd ending)

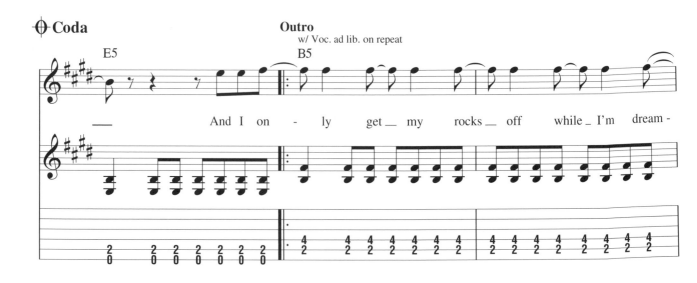

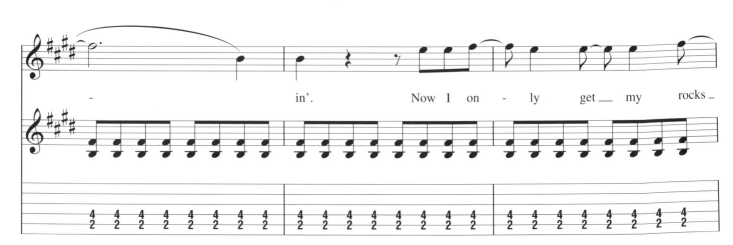

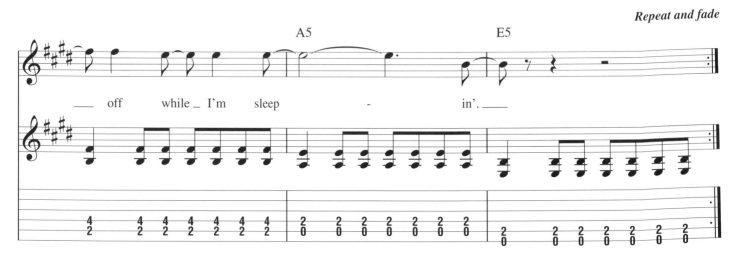

Additional Lyrics

3. I'm zipping through the days at lightning speed.
Plug in, flush out and fight a fucking feed.

Pre-Chorus 2. Heading for the overload,
Splattered on a dusty road.
Kick me like you kicked before;
I can't even feel the pain no more.

4. The sunshine bores the daylights out of me.
Chasing shadows, moonlight mystery.

Pre-Chorus 3. Heading for the overload,
Splattered on a dirty road.
Kick me like you kicked before;
I can't even feel the pain no more.

Runnin' Down a Dream

Words and Music by Tom Petty, Jeff Lynne and Mike Campbell

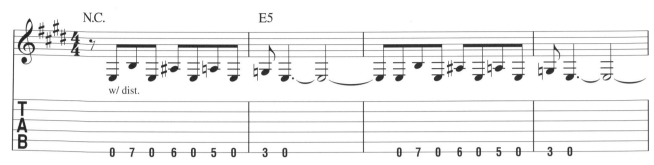

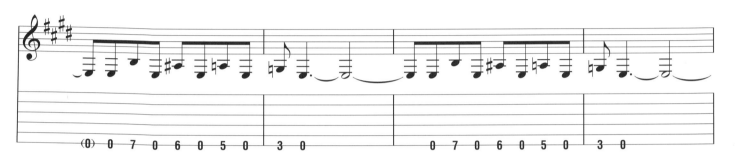

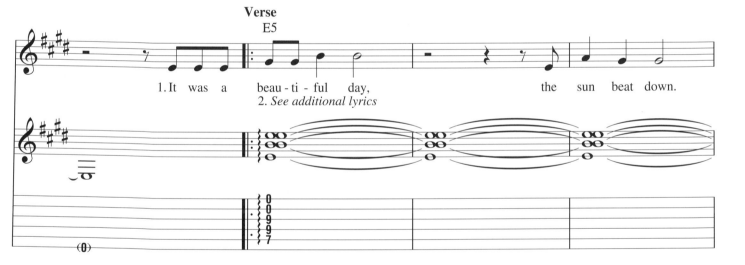

1. It was a beau-ti-ful day, the sun beat down.
2. *See additional lyrics*

I had the ra-di-o on. I was driv-in'.

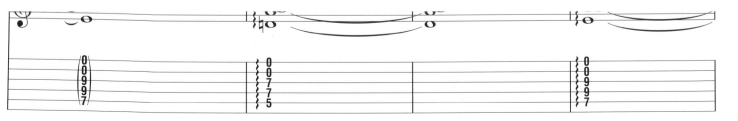

some - thin' good   wait - in' down this road.   I'm

pick - in' up   what - ev - er's   mine.   I'm

Chorus

run - nin' down a dream ___   that nev - er would come to me. ___

Additional Lyrics

2. I felt so good, like anything was possible.
   Hit cruise control, and rubbed my eyes.
   The last three days, and the rain was unstoppable.
   It was always cold, no sunshine.

Smoke on the Water

Words and Music by Ritchie Blackmore, Ian Gillan, Roger Glover, Jon Lord and Ian Paice

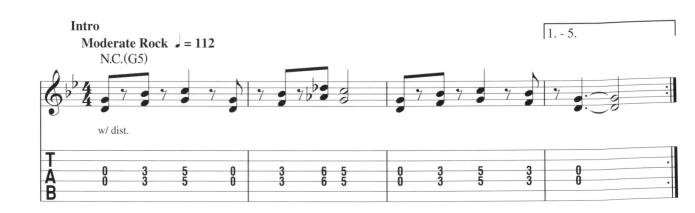

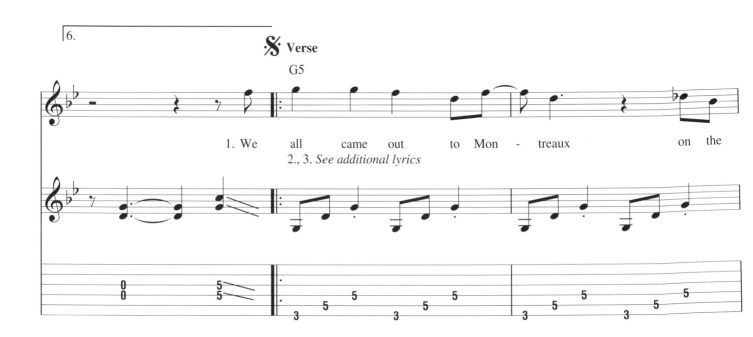

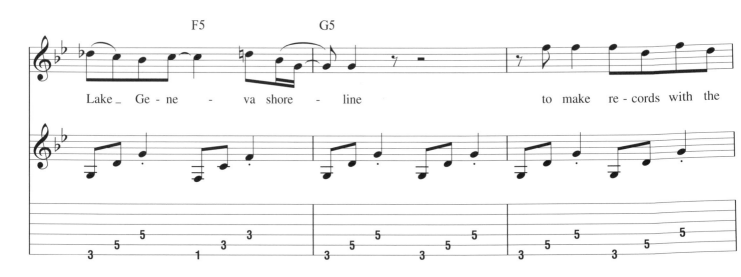

wa - ter,　　　a fire ___ in the sky. ___

To Coda ⊕

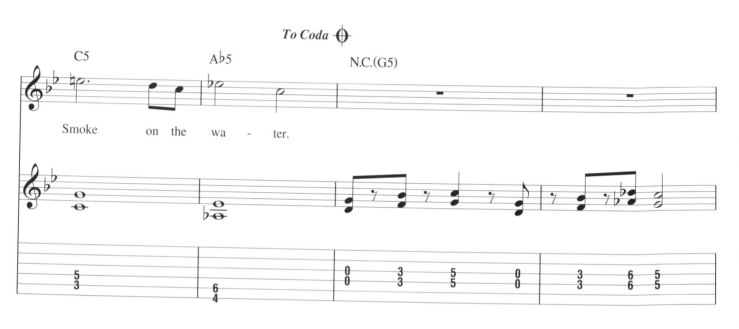

Smoke　　　on the wa - ter.

Guitar Solo

Additional Lyrics

2. They burned down the gambling house,
   It died with an awful sound.
   A Funky Claude was running in and out,
   Pulling kids out the ground.
   When it all was over, we had to find another place.
   It seemed we would lose the race.

3. We ended up at the Grand Hotel,
   It was empty, cold and bare.
   But with the Rolling truck Stones thing just outside,
   Making our music there.
   With a few red lights, a few old beds
   We made a place to sweat.
   No matter what we get out of this,
   I know, I know we'll never forget.

Strutter

Words and Music by Paul Stanley and Gene Simmons

1., 3. I know __ a thing or two a - bout __ her.
2. *See additional lyrics*

Coda 1

Guitar Solo

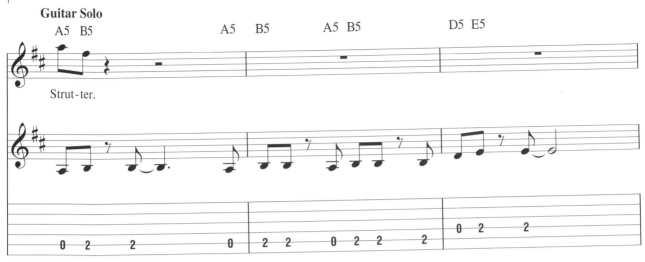

Strut-ter.

 Coda 2

Outro-Guitar Solo

Strut-ter.

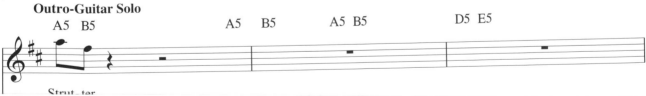

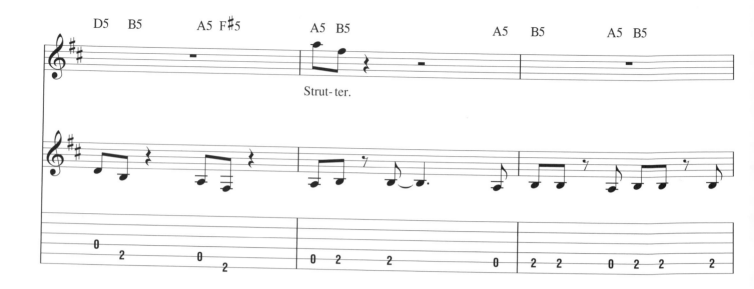

Strut- ter.

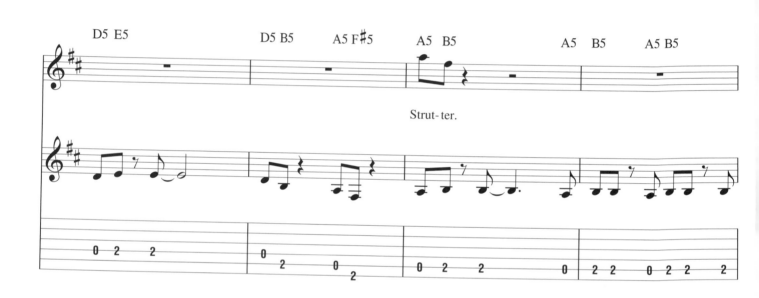

Strut- ter.

Additional Lyrics

2. She wears her satin like a lady.
   She gets her way just like a child.
   You take her home and she says, "Maybe, baby."
   She takes you down and drives you wild.

Up Around the Bend

Words and Music by John Fogerty

1. There's a place up a-head and I'm go - in'
2., 3., 4. *See additional lyrics*

just as fast as my feet can fly. Come a - way, come a - way

if you're go - in', leave the sink - in' ship be - hind.

Chorus

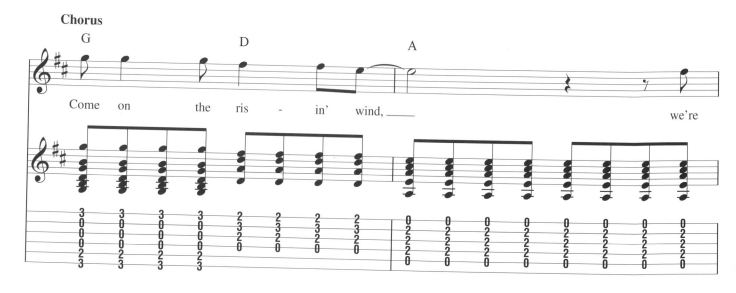

Come on the ris - in' wind, _____ we're

4th time, To Coda ⊕

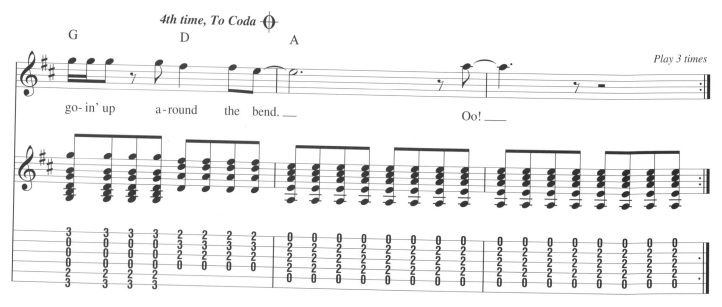

Play 3 times

go- in' up a - round the bend. __ Oo! __

Interlude

Guitar Solo

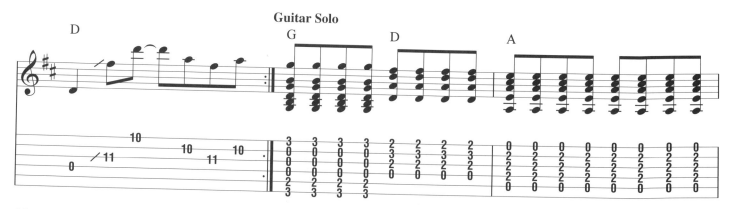

Additional Lyrics

2. Bring a song and a smile for the banjo.
   Better get while the gettin's good.
   Hitch a ride to the end of the highway

3. You can ponder perpetual motion,
   Fix your mind on a crystal day.
   Always time for a good conversation,
   There's an ear for what you say.

4. Catch a ride to the end of the highway
   And we'll meet by the big red tree.
   There's a place up ahead and I'm goin';
   Come along, come along with me.

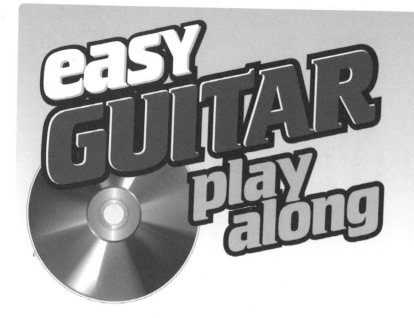

The *easy GUITAR play along*® Series

features streamlined transcriptions of you[r] favorite songs. Just follow the tab, liste[n] to the CD to hear how the guitar shoul[d] sound, and then play along using th[e] backing tracks. The CD is playable on an[y] CD player, and is also enhanced to includ[e] the Amazing Slowdowner technology s[o] Mac and PC users can adjust the recording to any tempo without changing the pitch[.]

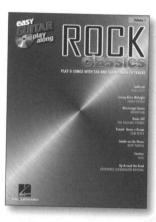

1. ROCK CLASSICS

Jailbreak • Living After Midnight • Mississippi Queen • Rocks Off • Runnin' Down a Dream • Smoke on the Water • Strutter • Up Around the Bend.

00702560 Book/CD Pack....$14.99

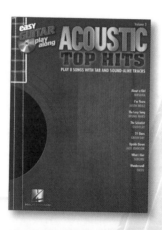

2. ACOUSTIC TOP HITS

About a Girl • I'm Yours • The Lazy Song • The Scientist • 21 Guns • Upside Down • What I Got • Wonderwall.

00702569 Book/CD Pack....$14.99

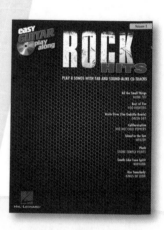

3. ROCK HITS

All the Small Things • Best of You • Brain Stew (The Godzilla Remix) • Californication • Island in the Sun • Plush • Smells like Teen Spirit • Use Somebody.

00702570 Book/CD Pack....$14.99

4. ROCK 'N' ROLL

Blue Suede Shoes • I Get Around • I'm a Believer • Jailhouse Rock • Oh, Pretty Woman • Peggy Sue • Runaway • Wake up Little Susie.

00702572 Book/CD Pack.....$14.99

5. ULTIMATE ACOUSTIC

Against the Wind • Babe, I'm Gonna Leave You • Come Monday • Free Fallin' • Give a Little Bit • Have You Ever Seen the Rain? • New Kid in Town • We Can Work It Out.

00702573 Book/CD Pack.....$14.99

HAL•LEONARD®
CORPORATION
7777 W. BLUEMOUND RD. P.O. BOX 13819
MILWAUKEE, WISCONSIN 53213

www.halleonard.com

Prices, contents, and availability subject to change without notice.